MIKE MILLS
CONTENTS

SHORT HISTORY
REPRESENTATIVE
IMAGE
PROJECT

Q & A

MIKE MILLS SHORT HISTORY

アーティストがこのような本に登場すると、たいてい その人は今まで自分がやって来たことをよく把握し、常に筋道の通った作品作りをしてきたように思われがちだがぼくはそう思われたくない。確かにぼくだってセールストークとして自分の作品がすべて意味を成しているように思わせたり、常に素晴らしい作品作りをしてきたように見立てたりしたことはある。でも本当は自分がなにをしているのか把握できないまま、目の前にある仕事を懸命にこなし、クライアントを満足させられる作品を作り、なんとかやって来ただけだ。その結果出来上がった作品が評価されぼくは喜びと驚きでいっぱいだ。これらは偶然の賜物

で、インドを探していたのにアメリカ大陸を発見してしまったような感じだ。みんなのコレクションの一部となっているかもしれないレコードカバー、長く着てもらったTシャツをデザインできたことを誇りに思っているし、それは自分にとっても最も大きな満足のいく仕事だ。子供の頃、退屈で孤独でなにかを成し遂げたい、世の中のことを知りたいと思ったとき、とにかく多くのドローイングを描いていた。自分のおもちゃ全部を慎重に描いたのも、ぼくが住んでいた世界に対応するための手段だった。高校のときに、自分の組んでいたバンドのフライヤーを作るためにグラフィックデザインを始めた。それ以前にも、

自分のスケートボードのための絵柄をスケッチしたりしていた。小学校6年の頃、ロックバンドのStyxやKansasのロゴの描き方を知っていることはぼくらにとってかっこいいことだった。中学生になると、StyxやKansasの両方とも描けるようになり、その他にもAdam and the AntsやなぜだかPILのロゴも描いたりしていた。みんなはぼくがいろんなパターンのロゴをうまく描けるという理由で好意を持ってくれたみたいだし彼らと話すきっかけにもなった。それに、ちょっと世の中にパンチを打てたような気がした。当時から比べてぼくはいったいどのくらい変わったのだろう？

I hate how these kind of books make it seems like the person, artist, subject knew what they were doing all along, or that it all makes perfect sense. I have to admit in selling myself to people I've often tried to make all my work make more sense than it does, to seem more on some magical trajectory than it is. Most of the time I had/have no idea what I'm doing, I'm just trying to get the job done, to get something approved by the client, to squeeze through some hole. And the work I have been totally surprised and excited about, the breakthroughs, came by

mistake you know, I was looking for India and I found America. I feel totally honored that I've done some record covers that people have in their collections and some shirts that people maybe wore out on dates that is the biggest accomplishment of all this work.

I used to draw a lot as a kid, when I was feeling bored-lonely-ambitious-whenever I tried to figure out the world - I would draw. I did meticulous drawings of all my toys, it was a way to cope with the world. I started doing graphics for my band's flyers in high school. Actually before that I used

to sketch graphics for my skateboards all the time. And I remember in 6th grade it was really cool to know how to draw the Kansas band logo, and I think Styx too. By Junior high I was drawing Kansas and Styx but also Adam and the Ants and somehow the P.I.L. logo too. People liked that I could draw a pretty good version of some logo, so it made it easier to talk to people and to have some clout in the world. How much has changed?

MIKE MILLS STUDIO / HOME   PHOTO: Todd Cole

REPRESENTATIVE IMAGE

"THE EXHAUSTED FALSE SELF"

「ヘトヘトに疲れた調子外れの自分」
ぼくの作品がパーソナルであればあるほど、または
なにかを啓示するようなものほど、ぼくをエキサイト
させる。アレン・ギンズバーグが自分の詩がみっと
もないと思ったときほど最もエキサイトすると言って
いるのを読んだことがある。彼が言うには、それは
自らが受け入れられないような自己のパーツを再び
集結させるようなものらしい。人はよく自分らしくあ
る代わりに、自分以外のなにかであろうとする時間
を多く過ごしているんじゃないかと思う。それは、ま
るでゲームをしているのか自分たちがゲームになっ
てしまっているとかという感覚なのかもしれない。で
も、それは最終的にはなにも得られないし、ほとほ
と疲れ果ててしまう。ぼくは、シリアスなことをシンプ
ルでちょっとバカっぽく見えるイメージとともに、シリア
スっぽくない感じで語るのが好きだ。ぼくは直感で仕
事をするタイプだが、このイメージスケッチはしばらく
はノートの中で寝かせておいた。それからしばらくして、
どうしてそのイメージが好きなのかとか、自分にとっ
てどんな意味があるのかなどを考え、そのときにな
ってやっとタイトルを付けるに至った。そして同時に
それはこの作品が完成したことを意味している。

More and more I am excited when my work is personal, somehow revealing. I read that Allen Ginsberg was most excited when his own poems embarrassed him, he said it was like re-integrating a part of yourself that you couldn't accept. I feel like just about everybody has spent a fair amount of time being something besides themselves, being anything but who we really are. It's like we're playing a game or we have become the game. But ultimately it's totally unrewarding, so you fall over dead with exhaustion. I've always liked to talk about serious things in a seemingly un-serious way, with images that seem very simple, stupid even. I think I also usually work intuitively, somehow I just sketched this image, and then it sat in my notebook for a while, and slowly I began to figure out why I liked it and what it meant to me and that's when I could title the piece, which is sort of finishing it for me.

1

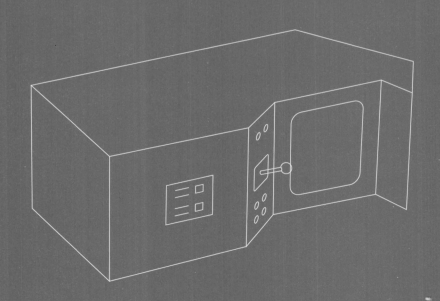

PROJECT 01 SKATEBOARDS

高校の時、自分のスケートボードを作ったり、そのグラフィックをしたりして、とにかくスケートとともに育った。13歳の頃、毎日のようにスケートパークで過ごし、そこでパンク・ミュージックのことを知り、惨めで受け入れがたい"普通の人々"とは違う人生があることを知った。これはちょっと自惚れて

いて、不完全に聞こえるかもしれないが、とにかくスケートこそ自分がどんな人間なのかを知るきっかけを作ってくれたと思っている。スケートパークに通うことで、クーパーユニオン（大学）に行ってアートとデザインを学ぶのと同じくらいのものを得られた。サンタ・バーバラの郊外出身のぼくは、わり

と無邪気な子供時代を過ごした。その後、正直いってぼくなんかよりよっぽどタフなLAのパンク・キッズと出会うことで、スタイルやみんなが求めるものがなにかを学べたし、自分が知っていたメインストリームでポップで従順で反ヒューマンで反個人的な文化から抜け出す方法を見つけられた。

I grew up skating, making my own boards and doing graphics for them in high school. I was 13 years old hanging out at skateparks everyday, that's when I learned about punk music and in general a way of life that wasn't the depressing and unaccepting land of "normal people." This sounds pretentious and lame but skating is

where I first started figuring out who I was. Hanging around in parks taught me as much about art/design as going to Cooper Union did. Coming from the suburb of Santa Barbara, and a fairly tame childhood, I was being exposed to all these tougher, more punk LA kids and to be honest, all these kids who were much stronger

individuals than I was - so I was learning about style, culturally fucking with people's expectations, and finding a way out of the mainstream-pop-conformist-anti-human-anti-individual culture that I thought was the only way.

1	RALPH NADAR SKATEBOARD FOR SUBLIMINAL	1996
2	PATTY HEARST SKATEBOARD FOR SUBLIMINAL	1995

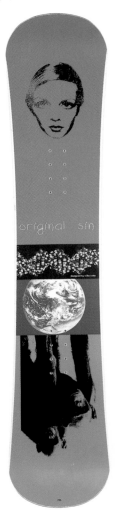

SUPREME T-SHIRTS

1995

PROJECT 02
MUSIC GRAPHICS

レコードやCDのカバーをデザインしたことは、自分にとって最良のことだったと思っている。レコードやCDのデザインを始めたのはぼくが25歳の時であったが、その頃はちょうどノーマルで責任感のある理性的なデザイナーでなければ仕事をもらえず、生きていけないのではないかと恐れていた時でもあった。しかし、レコードやCDカバーの仕事はすべてイメージだけの世界だったし、理性的なコミュニケーションもいらなかったから、とにかく自由に仕事ができた。ただバンドメンバーたちと仕事をするのは、いいこともあるけどストレスも溜まってしまう。自分が思っているかっこいいカバーのアイデアとはまったく関係のないテイストやニーズや不安などを持ち込まれ、それに基づいたカバー作りをしな

ければならない。カバーデザインが面白いのは、自分のテイストの範疇外のものからアイデアを引っ張る必要があるところだ。自分がクールと思ったこともめちゃくちゃになったりするけど、結果的にそれはいいものにつながると思う。とにかく、ぼくが仕事をしたすべてのバンドは、ぼく自身がいろんなアプローチをする手助けになった。当時、友人で「フィクション的なテイスト」を持ちたいと言った女のコがいた。つまり、ひとつのスタイルや見た目がほかより良いとかもっと価値があるということではなく、すべてはフィクションであり、ストーリーであるということだ。だからこそ、どんなものも作り上げられるということだ。そしてぼくもそうありたいと思っている。

Doing record/CD covers is one of the best things that happened to me. I was about 25 when I started doing them, and at the time I was afraid I was going to have to be more of a normal-responsible-rational designer to have a job and earn a living. But CD covers are all images, no rational communication, so it allowed me to be very free. Working with bands is totally great and totally frustrating. They come to a cover with all these strange issues, tastes, needs, fears, that have nothing to do with your idea of a good

cover. Part of this is great cause they always force you out of your own taste, they fuck up what you thought was so "cool" about yourself, which is ultimately really good. So all the bands I worked with helped me be really diverse. I had a friend at this time who used to say she wanted to "fictionalize taste," you know, not believe that any certain style or look was better or more valuable, it's all a fiction - a story - so you can make up anything. I tried to be like that.

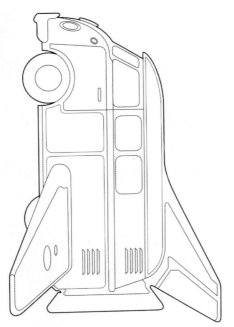

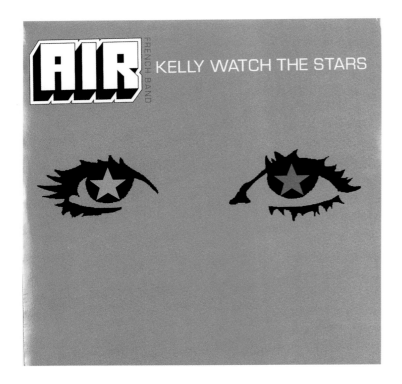

1	2		
3	4		

1   AIR, MOON SAFARI PROMO CD   1998

2   AIR, MOON SAFARI CD   1998

3   AIR, KELLY WATCH THE STARS SINGLE   1999

4   AIR, SEXY BOY 12" SINGLE   1998

AIR PLAYGROUND LOVE

Sung by Gordon Tracks

Taken from the Original Motion Picture Score for The Virgin Suicides

1

AIR, PLAYGROUND LOVE 7" SINGLE   2000

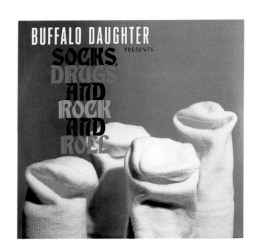

1 9MM
2 SHUT UP
3 BUTTER OF 69
4 DICK SERIOUS
5 HOW DO I RELAX
6 IT'S THE RAGE
7 MONO LISA
8 WHAT ARE YOU WEARING
9 SEX SYMBOL
10 DEGOBRAH
11 HARD TO HOLD
12 BUTTERFUCKER

PRODUCED BY
RUSSELL SIMINS, JAMEY STAUB
AND YUKA HONDA

Ⓟ©1996 GRAND ROYAL P.O. BOX 26689 L.A., CA 90026

WWW.GRANDROYAL.COM

"Guaranteed Every Time"

7 58148-0029-1 1

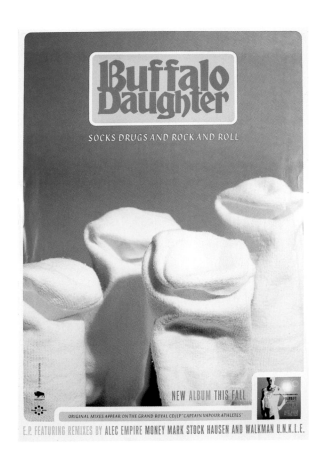

	1		1	ELEKTRA NEW RELEASE BOOK	1994
2	3	4	2	BUFFALO DAUGHTER POSTER	1997
			3	BLUES EXPLOSION POSTER	1995	PHOTO: Glenn E.Friedman
			4	SONIC YOUTH POSTER	1995

Sonic Youth Washing Machine

1	2	
		3

1	CIBO MATTO POSTER	1996
2	ELEKTRA NEW RELEASE BOOK	1994
3	SUMMERSAULT TOUR T-SHIRT	1996

SUMMERSAULT

PROJECT 03
PATTERNS AND IMAGES

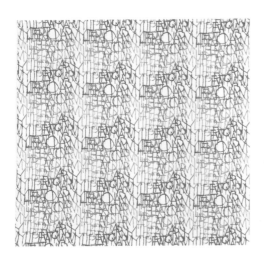

母親がVera社製スカーフのトラベリング・セールス
レディだったので、ぼくは実家にあった母親が好き
なタイプの絵柄パターンを見ながら育った。ぼくは
それらのデザインが好きだったし、できれば自分も
パターンを作ってみたいと思っていた。友人のミッ
シェル・ロックウッドから、彼女のブランド
「MATERIAL」のためにパターンをデザインしてほ
しいと依頼があった。そのときぼくは、マントラの
繰り返しのようにひとつのアイデアに取り付かれ

ていた。それは「リピートされるパターン」というイ
メージだったのだが、この仕事はRam Dassという
人物の「Be Here Now（今ここにいて）」という本に
影響された。Ramはヒッピー世代の伝説的な人物
で、その本にはRamによるいろいろなグラフィック
が載っていた。実は、カリフォルニアに引っ越して
以来、ぼくはヒッピーのことばかり考えている。ミ
ッシェルのためにデザインしたパターンの一つに
「Liberation Army（解放軍）」と書いたものを繰り返

して使用したけど、自分にとってヒッピーとは解放
の最前線にいる人たちを意味するんだ。ミッシェル
はまさにそういった人物だったし、そんなグループ
にぼくも参加したかった。これらのパターンのデザ
インは、あまりあれこれ考えないで、素早く作業を
行った。ぼくの場合、考えすぎるとだいたい凝りす
ぎて思わせぶりでスマートすぎるものができてしま
う。だから、常日頃からあまり何も考えないように
自分を持っていくように心がけているんだ。

My mother was a traveling saleswoman for Vera
Scarves, so I grew up with her patterns all
around the house. I always loved those designs
and wanted to do patterns. My friend Michelle
Lockwood asked me to do some for her clothing
line MATERIAL. I got very into the idea that these
repeating patterns were like repeating mantras.

This work was influenced a lot by Ram
Dass'book Be Here Now, a total hippie legend
with great info and graphics, and since I moved
to California I'm obsessed with hippies. One of
the patterns I did for Michelle said "Liberation
Army" over and over again to me the hippies
were a liberation front, that's what Michelle is,

that_s the army I'd like to join. Most of these were
just done really fast without thinking too much.
When I think too much my work gets really fussy,
pretentious, too "smart." I'm always trying to trick
myself into not thinking any more.

1			
2	1	MATERIAL PATTERN	2001
	2	MATERIAL POSTER	2001

LOVE

LIBERATION ARMY

LOVE
LOVE LOVE LOVE LOVE
LOVE LOVE

MATERIAL Fall & Winter Collection 2001

Illustrated by MIKE MILLS

DONT BE AF DONT BE AF
RAID TO SA RAID TO SA
Y THE WO Y THE WO
RDS POSIT RDS POSIT
IVE ENERGY IVE ENERGY

DONT BE AF DONT BE AF
RAID TO SA RAID TO SA
Y THE WO Y THE WO
RDS POSIT RDS POSIT
IVE ENERGY IVE ENERGY

1	1

FIGHTAGAI
NST THER
ISING TIDE
OF CONFO
RMITY.

FIGHTAGAI
NST THER
ISING TIDE
OF CONFO
RMITY.

FIGHTAGAI
NST THER
ISING TIDE
OF CONFO
RMITY.

FIGHTAGAI
NST THER
ISING TIDE
OF CONFO
RMITY.

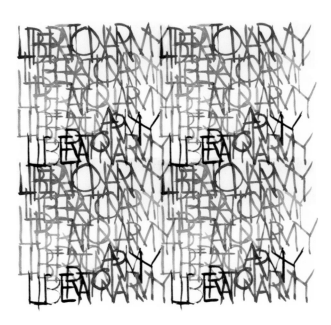

UNCONSCIOUS UNCONSCIOUS
UNCONSCIOUS UNCONSCIOUS
UNCONSCIOUS UNCONSCIOUS
UNCONSCIOUS UNCONSCIOUS
UNCONSCIOUS UNCONSCIOUS
UNCONSCIOUS UNCONSCIOUS
UNCONSCIOUS UNCONSCIOUS
UNCONSCIOUS UNCONSCIOUS
UNCONSCIOUS UNCONSCIOUS
UNCONSCIOUS UNCONSCIOUS
UNCONSCIOUS UNCONSCIOUS
UNCONSCIOUS UNCONSCIOUS

YOU WHOM MUST LEAVE EV
ERYTHING YOU CANNOT
CONTROL. IT STARTS WITH
YOUR FAMILY BUT SOON
COMES ROUND TO YOUR
SOUL WELL I'VE BEEN WHERE
YOUR HANGING AND
I THINK I KNOW HOW YOU'RE
PINNED WHEN YOUR NOT HELP
ING HOLY YOUR LONLINES
SAYS THAT YOU'VE SINNED.

YOU WHOM MUST LEAVE EV
ERYTHING YOU CANNOT
CONTROL. IT STARTS WITH
YOUR FAMILY BUT SOON
COMES ROUND TO YOUR
SOUL WELL I'VE BEEN WHERE
YOUR HANGING AND
I THINK I KNOW HOW YOU'RE
PINNED WHEN YOUR NOT HELP
ING HOLY YOUR LONLINES
SAYS THAT YOU'VE SINNED.

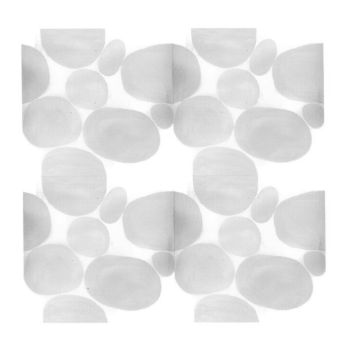

	2
1	3
	2

1	MARC JACOBS LIPS	1996
2	MARC JABOBS SCARVES	1996
3	MARC JACOBS NEON LOGO	1996

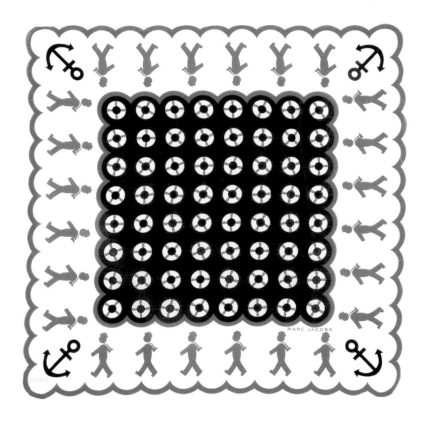

MARC JACOBS

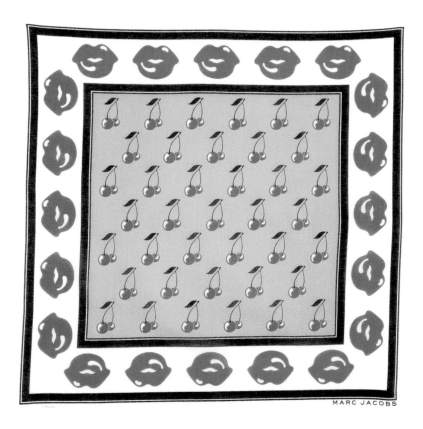

PROJECT 04
FASHION GRAPHICS

ぼくが成長していく過程で軸だったものがパンクス
とスケーターで、パンクスとスケーターというのは最
もファッションのとりこになっている人種だ。だから
ぼくもファッションおたくと言えるだろう。例えば、T
シャツはぼくにとってとても大切なもので、それはぼ
くの人生を通して常に存在していた。中学の時だっ
たか、「Talking Heads 77」と描かれたTシャツを着
ていたら、そのシャツのおかげでパンクが存在する
前の時代にパンキッシュでキュートな女のコに声を
かけられたのを覚えている。ぼく自身、10年から15
年前のTシャツをまだ持っていたりするのだが、その
間に大切なことやバカなこと、良かったことなどが
いろいろと起こった。だから、Tシャツをデザインす
ることは誰かの人生のパーソナルな部分になるもの
を作るということかもしれないわけで、そのことは光
栄なことだと思っている。デイジー・ヴォン・ファース
とキム・ゴードンが立ち上げたX-girlの仕事はとても
楽しかった。「インターナショナル・ビートニク」とか
「トラベル」などと彼女たちからテーマを投げてもら
い、それを受けてぼくはデザイン作業に取り掛かっ
ていった。あの仕事のおかげで、俳句みたいにほん
の小さなメッセージでもいいからTシャツの中にメッ
セージを入れることの面白みがわかるようになった。
それと、人とコミュニケートするのにこういったテー
マを持つことはすべての作業のベースになったし、
なにか言いたいこともできた。それと、シンプルなテ
ーマみたいなものを持つことは、自分のデザインが
ヴィジュアル的なマスターベーションで終わってしま
う不安からも救ってくれたと思っている。最近はと
にかく壁にぶち当たるとなにかテーマを決めていろ
いろ試みるようにしているんだ。

Let's admit that punkers and skaters, both of
which were central to my growing up, are the
biggest fashion slaves there are. So I guess I'm a
fashion head. I think T-shirts are super important.
They have been in my life - I can remember the
Talking Heads 77 shirt I got in Junior High and
how that really cute punk-before-there-was-punk
girl talked to me because of it. I have some shirts
that are 10 even 15 years old, things I've worn
while all sorts of important, stupid, good things
happened to me. So it's an honor making shirts,
making something that has the potential to be a
personal part of someone's life. Working for X-
girl, Daisy Von Furth and Kim Gordon was very
fun. They would come in with these themes like
"International beat-nick," or "travel" and I would
come up with a bunch of designs. I think this
work helped me figure out how much I like to
make little messages, even if they are tiny like a
haiku poem. But having these themes to
communicate gave me something to base
everything on, something to say, the simple
themes helped me feel like it's not all just visual
masturbating which is my biggest fear. Now days
when I'm stuck I always try to think of a theme to
play with.

1   LIVING DOLL POSTER   1994

2   X-GIRL ORIGINAL POSTER   1994

1	X-GIRL CORTINA	1995
2	X-GIRL YE OLDE LOGO	1996
3	X-GIRL DOT LOGO	1996
4	X-GIRL LIGHT BRIGHT LOGO	1995
5	X-GIRL MARCO POLO LOGO	1995

1	
	2

| 1 | X-GIRL HANG TAG FACES | 1994 |
| 2 | X-GIRL OUI | 1996 |

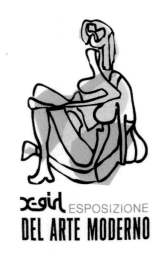

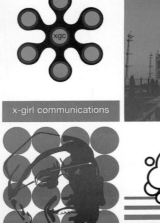

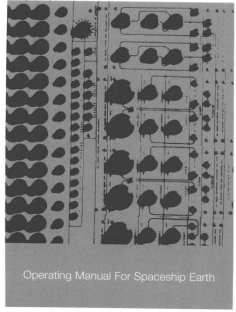

Operating Manual For Spaceship Earth

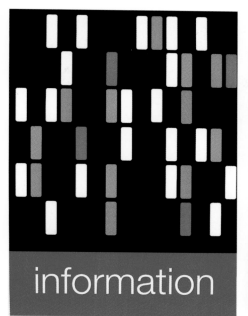

information

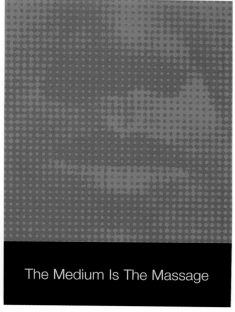

The Medium Is The Massage

cinema

travel

music

science

In Cold Blood

clothes for girls

TG-170 TG-170
170 ludlow street 995-8660   170 ludlow street 995-8660

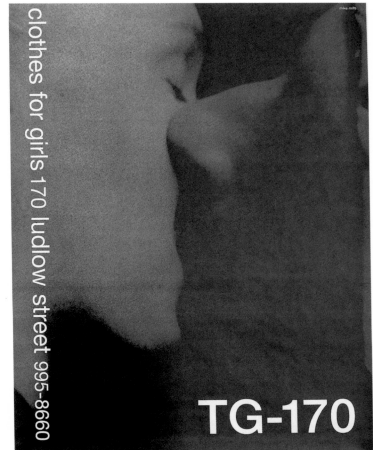

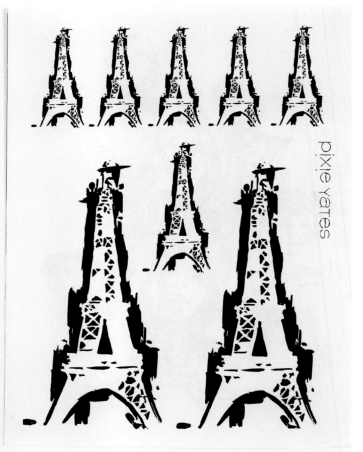

1	1

Pixie Yates fashion clip art book by mm/96

Pixie Yates

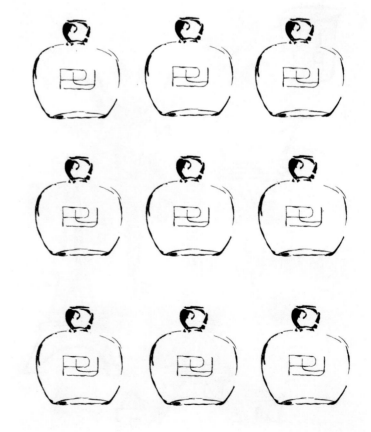

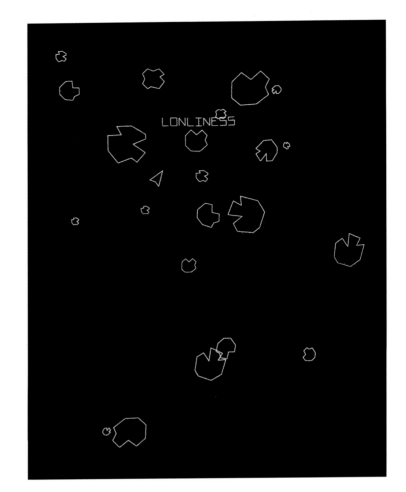

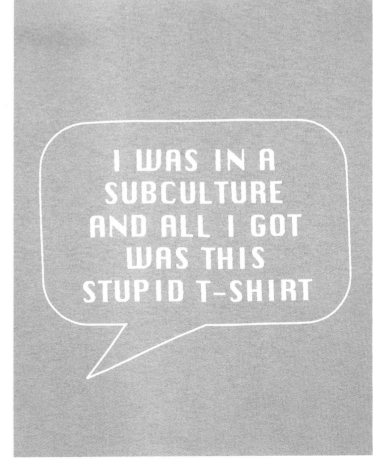

PROJECT 05 PHOTO EDITORIAL

ほとんどのグラフィックデザインは好きでない。凝りすぎているし、トレンドを追っているし、キュートすぎるし、クレバーすぎる。同じ理由で自分の多くの作品にも不満を感じたりする。トレンディーで、スタイリッシュで、底も浅く、なにも意味がないように見えるからだ。結局、ぼくがどんなにがんばっても「見た目の良さ」という問題にぶち当たるし、そこがぼくを悩ませる。自分のデザインやアートの中でも、なにかを語りかけ、なにかを含んで、なにか人とコミュニケートするものが好きだ。壁にスプレーで描いた作品は（これはグラフィティとも思わないし、もしそうだとしてもぜんぜん出来の良くないグラフィティだと思う）、一つのメッセージを凝縮したものだ。タイポグラフィ自体の出来も良くないけど、そういった方が逆に良かったりする。それに法を犯すことはなかなかロマンティックだったりするしね。

I have to admit, most graphic design I don't like. It seems so fussy and trend-oriented, too-cute, too clever. I have a hard time with a lot of my own work because of this, it just seems so trendy and stylish and shallow and nothing sometimes. No matter how hard I try it really just comes down to "looking cool" which drives me crazy. I guess I'm most happy when I feel like my design/art stuff is saying something, has some content, is communicating with people. With the writing on wall stuff (I don't think of it as graffiti or if it is graffiti it's pretty lame and pretentious and bad graffiti) it's just reduced to a message, my type isn't even that good which I love. And, there is something very romantic about breaking the law.

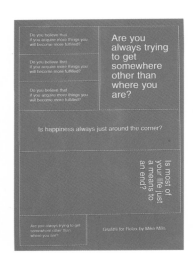

		1	RELAX STICKERS	2002
	2	2	GAS DVD "MIKE MILLS Let's be human beings"	2002
1			Graffiti: Mike Mills Photo: Todd Cole	
			Concept: Mike Mills and Maximilla Lukacs.	

Four Films By Mike Mills

WHO AM I?

PROJECT 06 PRINTED MATTER / POSTER

アートスクールに行っていた頃、アートやアーティストやギャラリーや美術館などを好きにならないようにしていた。それらはすべて近眼的で近親相姦的で複製可能で思わせぶりで排他的だったしそんなに興味をそそられなかった。それにアートはそれを知る内輪だけのものに属しているように見えたし。とはいいつつも、そんなぼくも自分がハッピーになれるようなものを作ってみたかった。当時、ディーン・ルーベンスキーとアレキサンダー・クゥという友人がいて、彼らはグラフィックデザインの世界に足を踏み入れていた。デザインの良さは公共を対象にしているところで、それにお金に対しスト

レートだしもったいぶったところがなかった。だからぼくも彼らを真似てデザインをやるようになったのだ。ぼくはずっとアートのようなものの作り方に興味があったけど、それを公共の場でもっとチープかつ簡単なやりかたで提示してみたかった。ミュージシャンが羨ましいと思うのは、彼らがなにかとてもパーソナルなものを作っても、それがとてもアートっぽくて、加えて比較的チープな値段で世界中で売れるようなものを作れることだ。ちなみに、ぼくがコレットのために作ったカードは、自分の作品を店で売るということへの試みだった。

When I went to art school I learned to not like art-artists-galleries-museums. It all seemed myopic, incestuous, duplicitous, pretentious, exclusive, not really interesting, just for those who already know. But, I still had to make things to be happy. I had some friends, Dean Lubensky and Alexander Ku who got into graphic design because it was public - straight up about money not as pretentious. I followed them. I have always been interested in ways to make something like art, but present it in a more public, cheap easy way. I envy musicians because they get to make something very personal, very much art, but it sells all over the world for relatively cheap amount. The cards I did for Colette are an attempt to make something and find a place for it in a store.

JANE GOODALL PRIMATOLOGIST

PRINCESS LEAH LEADER OF THE REBEL ALLIANCE

JON SPENCER ROCK AND ROLL SINGER

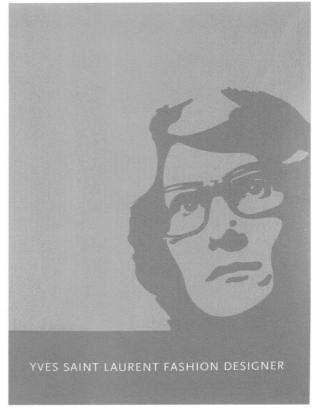

YVES SAINT LAURENT FASHION DESIGNER

1	2	1	COLETTE BIOGRAPHY CARDS	1998
		2	THE ARCHITECTURE OF REASSURANCE BOOK	1999	PHOTO: Susanna Howe

THE ARCHITECTURE OF REASSURANCE

PROJECT 07
ART EXHIBIT

ぼくは偽善者だ。というのも、アートシーンやギャラリーなどを批判しつつも、自分の好きな作品のいくつかは実はギャラリーで展示した。ぼくは、展示するところがアーロン・ローズと彼のアレッジド・ギャラリーでなかったなら、決してギャラリーで展示などしなかったと思う。彼のギャラリーは、ちょっと遊びに行ってたむろする場で、退屈した連中がロドロウ・ストリートでビールでも飲みながら、かわいい女のコが来るのを待っているようなところ

だった。アーロンを通して多くの素晴らしいアーティストたちに出会い、そして大いに刺激を受けた。ぼくがショウのために制作した好きな作品に『これが最後だと知ったらきみはどうする』というのがある。これは、基本的には人が死ぬこと、傷つきやすいこと、人の変化やこの世からいなくなってしまうことなどをテーマにした作品だ。ニューヨークに住んでポップアート的なことをするのではなく、LAに移り住んで自分の庭で時間を過ごしながら、自

らのことを考えたりして、もっとパーソナルな仕事の仕方をするきっかけを作った作品でもある。それと、これはぼく自身が作品を作ることを止めるという試みにも繋がった。そうすることで何かアイデンティティを与えてくれると思ったし、この世の中で自分に何か役割を与えてくれると感じたからだ。そして、自分をより良く知り、啓示し、もっと感じやすくし、自身を感情的に吐き出せるような作品を作りたいと思うようになったんだ。

So I'm hypocritical because I always criticized the normal art scene and gallery world but I have to admit that some of my favorite work has been for galleries. I don't think I would have shown in Galleries if it weren't for Aaron Rose and the Alleged gallery. It was really more of a hangout, a bunch of board guys drinking beer on Ludlow Street hoping some nice girl would come along. I

met so many great artists through Aaron that totally inspired me. Some of my favorite pieces I did for a show called "what will you do now that you know this is the end." It's about people dying basically, vulnerabilities, people changing and going away. I think it marks when I started doing more personal work, not just living in New York and being sort of a pop-artist, but living in LA and

hanging out in my garden and actually admitting things about myself. I think it's part of my attempt to stop making work because it gives you some identity, some play in the world, and start making stuff in an attempt to know yourself more, reveal more, be more vulnerable, sort of emotionally out yourself.

| | | 1 | VISUAL SAMPLER | 1996 |
| 1 | 2 | 2 | INTIMACY AND LONLINESS | 1996 |

intimacy and lonliness

portrait of a mannequin

Individuality

Stickers w/ sociological theme

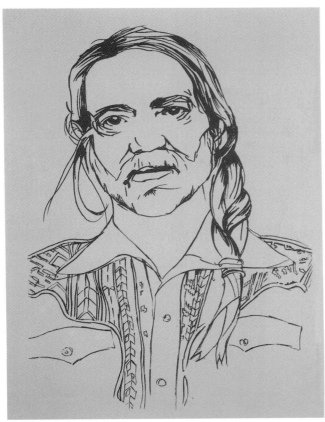

	1	BONJOUR TRISTESSE	1996
1 2	2	MONKEY	1996
3 4	3	WILLIE NELSON	1992
	4	SAD	1996

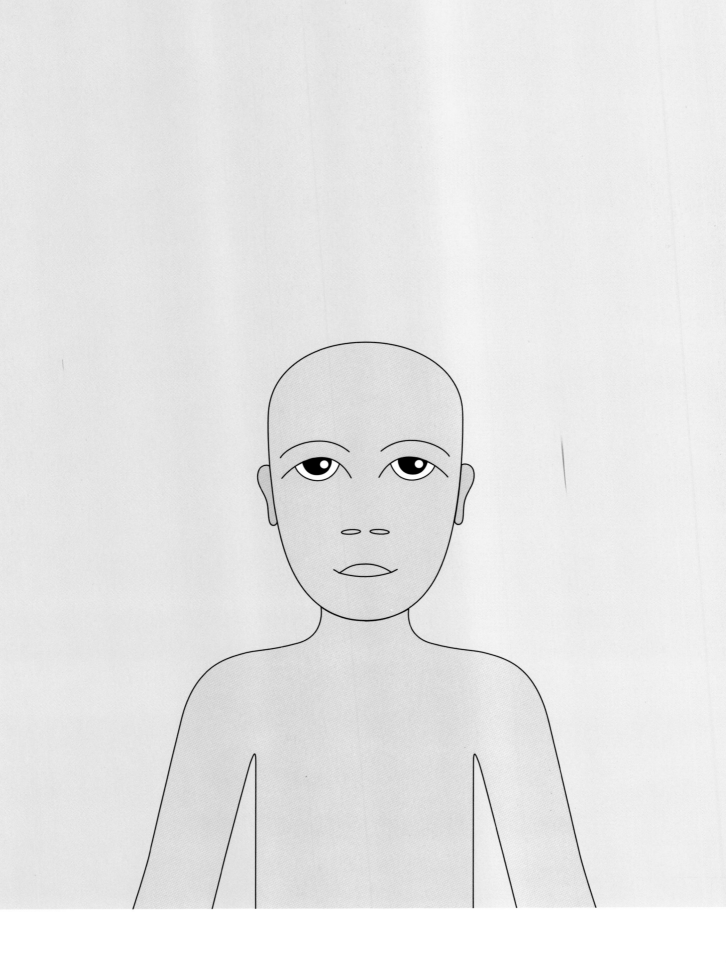

EVERY FACE THE SAME   1998

1

1   1

just lines, not a bear.

categories of thought

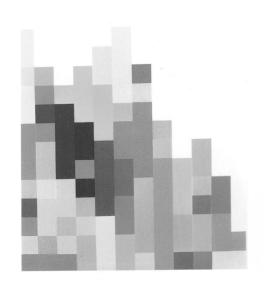

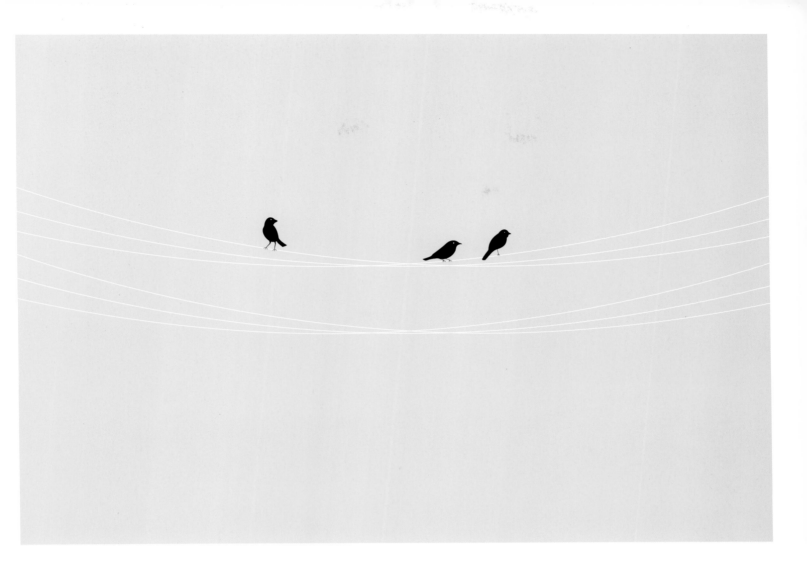

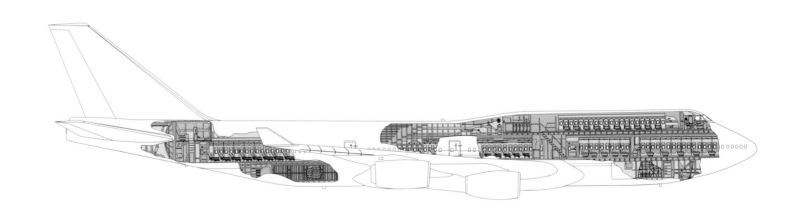

1	2	
	3	

1	ALL OF US / PARKING LOT	2000
2	ANGELS ON THE WIRE	2000
3	PLANE FULL OF GHOSTS	2000

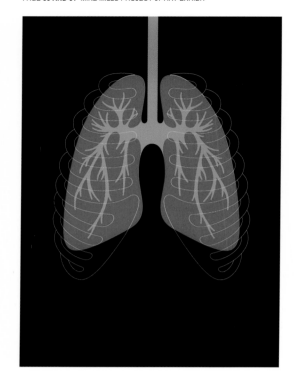

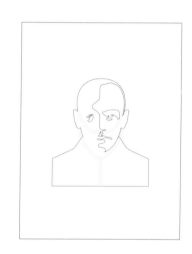

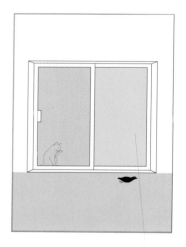
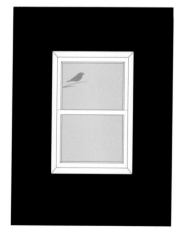

1	2	
3	4 5 6	
7 8 9 10		

1	VULNERABILITES / BREATHING	2000
2	SLEEPING GIRL	2000
3	ANGEL ON THE STOPLIGHT	2000
4	DEAD DOG	2000
5	ORDER	2000
6	VULNERABILITES / LUNGS	2000
7	DEAD BIRD	2000
8	THE OTHER SIDE	2000
9	CHILDHOOD	2000
10	VULNERABILITES / SHOE	2000

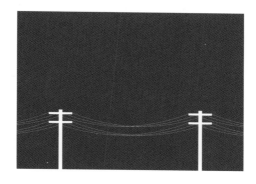

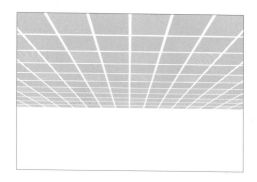

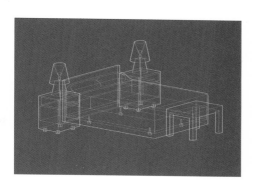

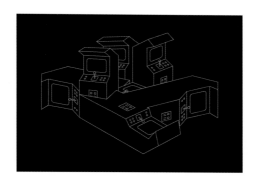

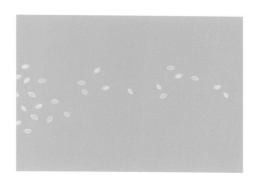

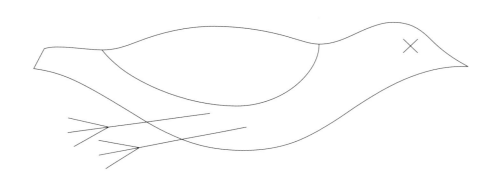

ANSWERS

THE DIRECTORS BUREAU

1) When you most feel the presence of "design" around you?
   Disneyland.
2) What is your favorite shape?
   Squares or rectangles.
3) What was your happiest moment in your work experience?
   When I saw my first poster on the street.
4) Please list up your 3 favorite colors.
   Changes daily: Today, pink, black and yellow.
5) What do you hate the most?
   Too much doubt/too much confidence.
6) Please list up your 3 favorite materials.
   Ink brush on denril, vellum, uni-ball pens in different colors, moleskine
   notebooks.
7) Where is your most favorite place?
   Mountains.
8) Please list up your 3 favorite designers.
   A.M. Cassandre, Quentin Fiore, Guy Dubord.
9) Please define the word "design".
   Putting things in some kind of order, except all forms of "order" are
   arbitrary and transient.
10) Please list up your 3 favorite words.
   Changes daily: Today, Stupid, Monsters, and Blood.